Table of Cont

A COLORFUL Garden

A garden is a special place. You can grow flowers, fruits, vegetables, or herbs in a garden. You can create a garden in a pot, your backyard, or at school.

SESAME STREET

GROW YOUR COLORS

Planting and Eating Healthy Foods with Sesame Street

Jennifer Cook

Lerner Publications ◆ Minneapolis

Alongside their friends from Sesame Street, young readers will learn the importance of growing and eating from a healthy garden. Elmo and all of his furry friends will first learn how to take care of plants, then watch them grow, and finally enjoy eating colorful fruits and vegetables.

Sincerely,
The Editors at Sesame Street Workshop

The colorful foods from the garden are delicious and good for you.

Eating colorful fruits and vegetables keeps me healthy!

GROWING Our Colors

Let's plant some seeds in the ground or in a pot with soil.

Me love when seeds grow into yummy carrots.

First, we dig a small hole in the dirt. We drop fruit or vegetable seeds in the hole.

I sprinkle the little seeds very carefully.

We cover the seeds with dirt and give them some water. Then the sun helps the seeds grow into plants.

I add more water
when the dirt gets
too dry.

What will grow in our colorful garden? There may be bright **RED** strawberries or tomatoes.

Maybe there will be yummy bell peppers for Elmo to eat!

We may dig up carrots or find **ORANGE** pumpkins on thick, green vines.

I love pumpkins!
I have pumpkins in my garden.

There could be **YELLOW** corn, summer squash, or even wax beans.

I like yellow
lemons.
They're sour!

Some vegetables and fruits are **GREEN**. Cucumbers are green. So are broccoli, honeydew, and snap peas.

I count one, two cucumbers.
Ah, ahh, ahhh!

Blueberries are **BLUE**
and grow on bushes.
Potatoes grow underground.

I love all berries, but blueberries are my favorite!

PURPLE eggplants and purple plums also grow in gardens.

I reach up high to get a plum!

Colorful, healthy foods are good for you. We love to plant them, care for them, and eat them!

What colors will you grow in your garden?

COLORFUL Fruit Salad

What You Need

- sliced melon, such as watermelon, cantaloupe, or honeydew
- berries, such as raspberries or blueberries
- other sliced fruit, such as pineapple, strawberries, red or green grapes, or kiwifruit

What You Do

1. Place bite-sized melon in a bowl.
2. Add fresh berries and other bite-sized fruit to the mix.
3. Toss the fruit salad with two big spoons.
4. You've built a healthy, colorful snack. Yummy!

Picture Glossary

garden: a place to grow flowers, fruits, vegetables, or herbs

herbs: leaves or other plant parts added to foods to make them taste better

seeds: small parts from plants that can grow into new plants

vines: long, curly stems

Read More

Gleisner, Jenna Lee. *Eating Healthy Foods*. Minneapolis: Tadpole Books, 2023.

Konstantinovskaya, Olga. *Big Book of Colorful Foods*. New York: Clever Publishing, 2022.

Schwartz, Heather E. *Cookie Monster's Foodie Truck: A Sesame Street Celebration of Food*. Minneapolis: Lerner Publications, 2020.

Photo Acknowledgments

SolStock/E+/Getty Images, p. 5; Baloncici/Getty Images, p. 6; GrapeImages//Getty Images, p. 8; Jupiterimages/The Image Bank/Getty Images, p. 10; kali9/E+/Getty Images, p. 12; Martinns/E+/Getty Images, p. 14; Hal_P/Shutterstock, p. 14 (inset); MNStudio/Shutterstock, p. 16; tanrock Gaphoto/Getty Images, p. 16 (inset); Suvit Maka/EyeEm/Getty Images, p. 18; romiri/iStock/Getty Images, p. 18 (inset); Goodboy Picture Company/Getty Images, p. 20; valentinrussanov/E+/Getty Images, p. 20 (inset); GraficallyMinded/Alamy, p. 22; Kyu Oh/Getty Images, p. 22 (inset); Miljan Živković/Getty Images, p. 24; AleksandarNakic/E+/Getty Images, p. 24 (inset); Ariel Skelley/Getty Images, p. 26; Africa Studio/Shutterstock, p. 29; Joanne Dale/Shutterstock, p. 30 (top); stockcreations/Shutterstock, p. 30 (third from botton); Ecaterina Glazcova/Shutterstock, p. 30 (second from bottom); vladispas/iStock/Getty Images, p. 30 (bottom).

Cover: Ariel Skelley/DigitalVision/Getty Images.

Index

To Sean & Gavin, You Color My World

Lerner Publications Company
An imprint of Lerner Publishing Group, Inc.
241 First Avenue North
Minneapolis, MN 55401 USA

For reading levels and more information, look up this title at www.lernerbooks.com.

Main body text set in Mikado a Medium.
Typeface provided by HVD.

Editor: Amber Ross **Designer:** Mary Ross
Lerner team: Martha Kranes

Library of Congress Cataloging-in-Publication Data

Names: Cook, Jennifer, 1975- author.
Title: Grow your colors : planting and eating healthy foods with Sesame Street / Jennifer Cook.
Description: Minneapolis : Lerner Publications, [2024] | Includes bibliographical references and index. | Audience: Ages 4–8 | Audience: Grades K–1 | Summary: "Growing your own fruits and vegetables is fun and good for you. Join Tamir, Abby, and the Sesame Street friends as they introduce young learners to the basics of planting a garden and eating healthy"— Provided by publisher.
Identifiers: LCCN 2023002092 (print) | LCCN 2023002093 (ebook) | ISBN 9798765604298 (library binding) | ISBN 9798765616420 (epub)
Subjects: LCSH: Gardening—Juvenile literature. | Colors—Juvenile literature. | Fruit—Juvenile literature. | Vegetables—Juvenile literature. | BISAC: JUVENILE NONFICTION / Cooking & Food
Classification: LCC SB457 .C655 2024 (print) | LCC SB457 (ebook) | DDC 635—dc23/eng/20230317

LC record available at https://lccn.loc.gov/2023002092
LC ebook record available at https://lccn.loc.gov/2023002093

ISBN 979-8-7656-2455-5 (pbk.)

Manufactured in the United States of America
1-1009274-51416-5/15/2023